Old ANNBANK and MOSSBLO

Including the lost villages of BURNBRAE, CRAIGHALL, TARHO

by

Denholm T. Reid

The bottom of the main street in Annbank looking north. On the right is the coal company's store, which incorporated the post office and reading room. Behind this building was a bowling green. Looking south from the store (i.e. towards the camera) one would have seen only open fields, with Annbank Farm just a few hundred yards up the road.

First published in the United Kingdom, 2005,
by Stenlake Publishing Ltd.
Telephone: 01290 551122
www.stenlake.co.uk
Printed by Cordfall Ltd., Glasgow, G21 2QA

ISBN 1 84033 347 2

ACKNOWLEDGEMENTS

The author is particularly indebted to Mary McKenna for the wealth of material she has gathered and generously made freely available, and for her encouragement; and to Tommy Wharrie for his enthusiasm, introductions, loan of material and time unstintingly given. Thanks are also due to all who assisted in various ways: their help is much appreciated. Mary Brown, Mossblown Library; Ellen Findlay; David Gourlay Snr; Robert Grieves; Terry Harrison; Jean Kennedy; Margaret Paschke; Stuart Rankin; John Roddie; staff of Carnegie Library, Ayr, Local History Department; and the many villagers (they know who they are) who shared their memories. Finally, a big thank you to Deirdre for her patience and support.

FURTHER READING

The books listed below were used by the author during his research. With the exception of *Mining: Ayrshire's Lost Industry*, none of them are available from Stenlake Publishing. Those interested in finding out more are advised to contact their local bookshop or reference library.

Arnot, R. P., *A History of the Scottish Miners*, 1955
Arthur, J., *Rambles on the Banks of the Ayr*, 1884
Hay, S., *Gathered Threads*, 1984
Hutton, G., *Mining: Ayrshire's Lost Industry*, 1996
Millar, A. H., *The Castles and Mansions of Ayrshire*, 1885 (reprinted 2004)
Paterson, J., *History of the Counties of Ayr and Wigton*, Vol. 1, 1863
Rankin, S. W., *G&SWR Association, Sou' West Profile No. 4, Ayr & Cumnock Branches*, 2000
Reid, W.; Close, R.; & Paschke, M., *Annbank School, 1903–2003*, 2003
Strawhorn, J. & Boyd, W., *The Third Statistical Account of Scotland: Ayrshire*, 1951

Ayrshire Archaeological and Natural History Society publications:

Broad, H., *Rails to Ayr*, Ayrshire Collections XIII, No. 3, 1981
McKerrell, T. & Brown, J., *Ayrshire Miners' Rows, 1913*, Ayrshire Collections XIII, No. 1, 1979
Paterson, B. E., *The Social and Working Conditions of the Ayrshire Mining Population, 1840–1875*, Ayrshire Collections X, 2nd series, 1972
Sleight, G. E., *Ayrshire Coal Mining and Ancillary Industries*, Ayrshire Collections VII, 2nd series, 1966
Wilson, J. P., *The Last Miller*, Ayrshire Monographs, No. 23, 2000

Left: At the top of the main street in Annbank. The road branching off to the left (ultimately to be known as Brocklehill Avenue) led to a three-quarter square of houses, opposite which was the former League Hall. This originally served as a place of worship for the Roman Catholic community, but later became the village hall. The road past the square ran close to the river and led to a former quarry, near where the football ground, Pebble Park, home of the local football team until 1949, was located. Looking straight on, about 30 homes form a row on one side of the road leading to Weston Crossroads. To the right a track (later Old School Brae) leads down to Weston School.

INTRODUCTION

In historical terms the villages of Annbank and Mossblown are modern, having been in existence little more than 150 years. Annbank district extends along the north bank of the River Ayr from close to the hone mill at Stair to Tarholm. The first recognisable local names to appear on maps are 'Montblawin' and 'Preuick Mill', recorded on Timothy Pont's map of *c.*1600.

Initially essentially an agricultural area, the district was transformed in the early part of the nineteenth century with the development of coal mining. Whereas there had formerly been many small shallow pits and surface 'ingaunees' scattered across the countryside, which coped with the demand for coal for domestic use and for small industrial processes such as lime kilns, major changes in the iron smelting industry brought about a huge requirement for coal. More and more industrial-scale pits opened up, which required more labour plus accommodation for the workers. Coalmasters found it necessary to provide company housing for their workforce and their families, and terraces of miners' rows soon sprung up across the county. While some were close to towns, many were in remote spots near to the pits. Examples included here are those at Burnbrae, Craighall, Tarholm and Woodside, all built and owned by mining companies.

The original village of Annbank was built between 1853 and 1863 by the mining company George Taylor & Co. It comprised 233 houses, mostly in a single street with the rows on either side. Conditions were very basic, with most of the houses having only one room and their occupants sharing dry closets outside. Prior to the arrival of these rows there had been little in the area save Annbank House (page 11) and Farm.

A waggonway ran from the nearby Enterkine Pit to Ayr Harbour, the export of coal to Ireland being extensive about this time. Soon a good rail network was developed and further branch lines followed to serve the increasing number of pits. In 1870 a line from Ayr to Mauchline was opened with a station known as Annbank Station, albeit situated some distance from the village. Two years later a line from Annbank Station to Cumnock followed.

Annbank Station developed as a community in its own right with housing around the station and on the road to Annbank. The opening up of Auchencruive 1, 2 and 3 Colliery led to the mining company William Baird & Co. building rows close by, and the colliery and rows became known as Mossblown after a local farm. Drumley Pit, situated close to Annbank Station, opened in the mid-1890s and the owners built two rows for its workers. Thus Annbank Station, Mossblown and Drumley became three separate communities, each with its own identity, although they were ultimately united and known as Mossblown. For simplicity's sake, if erroneously, 'Mossblown' will be used in this book where perhaps the old 'Annbank Station' is more accurate.

The conditions miners had to work in were bad, and often their living quarters were also poor. Houses were cramped, water had to be collected from pumps or barrels, and toilet arrangements were spartan. Company-run 'truck' stores stocked everything that the workers could need but clawed back men's wages as soon as they were paid. They also allowed people to run up large debts which made them behoven to the company. The truck system was cruel.

Nonetheless, people got on with their lives. Leisure activities for miners and their families tended to involve the whole community, living as they did in close-knit proximity. Working in dirty, dangerous and dark conditions, miners frequently got involved in outdoor activities. Individual pursuits included running, cycling, going walks and fishing, while others preferred greyhound racing or keeping homing pigeons ('doos'). A popular game was quoiting, where iron rings were thrown over a peg, and it was claimed that the old quoiting ground at the top of Weston Brae attracted the best quoiters in Scotland.

Even the smallest hamlet had a football team and there was friendly rivalry between villages. Annbank's team of the 1890s – the 'White Brigade' – became legendary with its successes, and there were many teams playing at junior and juvenile levels in the first half of the twentieth century. Annbank also had a bowling green as far back as the late 1890s. After a hiatus of seventeen years a new green opened in 1938 and the club has produced many champions at national and international level.

Music in various forms also provided entertainment. Most villages had talented exponents of fiddle or 'squeeze box', while others enjoyed choirs organised by, amongst others, the Co-operative Society. Over the years there have been pipe bands which often played at events across the county.

Although many miners left school at an early age, there were those who went to evening classes or were self-taught. Before the advent of the organised council library there was a reading room next to the store in Annbank and one in the Co-operative building in Mossblown. Many have a love for the works of Burns and the communities featured in this book have produced their fair share of 'miner' poets.

Over the years the area's religious needs have been well catered for. In Annbank there was initially a Presbyterian church (the 'Iron Kirk') which, after being destroyed by fire, was replaced by the still-in-use building on the Annbank Road. In Mossblown there was a UF church. The Roman Catholic community originally had to use the old school in Annbank and later an 'iron' chapel. In 1898 the congregation moved to the fine new Chapel of St Ann in Mossblown. Different factions of the Brethren had halls in both Annbank and Mossblown.

Annbank was initially served by Weston School, but the village's Roman Catholic children moved when the new St Ann's Church (which doubled as a school) was built, and a new school was opened in Mossblown in 1903. Later, in 1931, St Ann's RC School opened.

Major changes in housing took place in the 1930s in Annbank, creating in effect a new village. The old rows were demolished, being replaced with new houses built in their backyards. Several new streets were also created. While all the old rows had belonged to the mining company, most of the new houses were owned by the county council, with some belonging to Bairds & Dalmellington Ltd. The village took on a whole new persona. Similarly in Mossblown the old rows were replaced by modern council houses as well as 'prefabs' built immediately after the Second World War. In the meantime the small hamlets of Burnbrae, Craighall, Woodside and Tarholm (pages 40–45) were deserted, their former occupants moving to modern housing elsewhere. Soon they were abandoned and demolished.

One by one the four pits that remained in the area in the 1940s closed, the miners being transferred elsewhere and ultimately to Killoch Colliery. Mossblown Pit was the last to go, closing at the end of 1960.

In 1951 the population of Annbank stood at around 2,000, with slightly fewer people living at Mossblown. By 1991 the figure had dropped to 925 for Annbank, while Mossblown's population had increased to 2,039. However, unemployment figures soon became a large proportion of the number of residents. Hotels that opened in Annbank and Mossblown enjoyed short-lived existences, while those industries that remained gradually ceased, and in general there was little source of employment for local people. Today some work in the retail trade, the care home employs several and the food processors on the Sandyford Road have a reasonable workforce – otherwise locals have to travel elsewhere to work. Mossblown has expanded recently with new private housing being built off the Mauchline Road.

Despite the downturn in the local economy over the past 50 years, the villages of Annbank and Mossblown are still held in great affection by locals, past and present, and the community spirit lives on.

Annbank's square was located midway up the main street, with half on one side and half on the other. Here washing is hanging out to dry after the rigours of the wash-house, one of which was situated on either side of the square.

Weston Avenue in the early 1930s, showing many changes from the earlier views seen on previous pages. The roadway has become just that, and is no longer a track as before, with a proper made-up surface and the addition of pavements. Telegraph poles and power lines have appeared and the water butts have gone – clearly piped water has been installed. However, something dramatic is happening: new houses have sprouted up behind the row beyond the square.

A closer view of these big changes. In the foreground things are pretty well as normal in the square, with washing hanging out on the lines close to the wash-house. However, in the background behind the row, new houses have been built, starting with the blocks which would become 51 & 49, 47 & 45 etc. Weston Avenue. In the days of the rows there were no official street names, and the houses would simply be known as, for instance, 51 Annbank.

This is all that remains of the old rows, the new houses having been built behind them. It was this system of building new houses in the backyards of the existing rows – which were then demolished – which led to Weston Avenue being described in the *Statistical Account* of 1951 as a 'wide boulevard'. The line of the original rows was kept, as was the central square (albeit at an angle), with several new streets of similarly designed houses added. Some of these belonged to Ayr County Council and others to Bairds & Dalmellington (later the National Coal Board). Thus, in Weston Avenue in 1935, odd numbers from 1–67 were built by Bairds & Dalmellington, with the county council owning odd numbers 69–123 and even numbers 2–104.

In 1871 a chapel of ease to Tarbolton was erected at the top of Annbank's School Brae. This 'temporary' building of corrugated iron, with walls lined with wood, soon became known as the 'Iron Kirk'. Prior to its erection villagers gathered to worship in the 'Auld Schule'. The Iron Kirk was later extended and could seat approximately 400, although this must have been quite a squeeze in the 70 or so pews. In the early hours of Tuesday 8 January 1901 tragedy struck, with the building being destroyed in a blaze thought to have been the result of fires being left on to prevent heating pipes from freezing (although some five years earlier 'trouble over the stove' had been reported, and perhaps this was a repetition of that trouble with drastic consequences). It was recorded that the only item to be salvaged was the minister's robe, although the reaction of Rev Alexander Cameron, ordained less than a year before, is unknown. Inevitably it was suggested that local children combed the smouldering embers in search of collection money which was then diverted from God's use.

Above: This august group of church managers, photographed in 1895, was appointed to administer the affairs of the Iron Kirk. Little did they know then the extent to which their management skills would be put to the test some five years later.

Back row: J. A. Clarke (colliery owner); W. Bell (surface worker); Thomas Murray (country joiner); Peter Watson (colliery cashier) *Front row:* James Boyd (baker); John 'Jake' McArthur (schoolmaster); Samuel Robertson (coal miner); Alexander Park (colliery oversman)

After the fire which destroyed the Iron Kirk the church managers met and resolved to build a replacement. By September that year sufficient funds had been raised to engage contractors for the new building. Among the benefactors to the new church were Mr James A. Clarke, the local coalmaster, who gifted £500, and his sisters Lily, Margaret and Elizabeth who provided for the church bell and a stained glass window. Peter Watson of High Drumley, the cashier of the colliery, and his wife donated a harmonium, pulpit bible and hymn book. The Laird of Enterkine, John Bell, decreed that no land of his would be given for a church at Annbank, but his counterpart at Auchencruive had no such scruples and a site was found on the road to Annbank Station, just past the Muirburn Bridge, known locally as the 'Sawmill Bridge', and where no undermining had occurred. The official opening service took place on 3 May 1903, conducted by the Moderator of the General Assembly of the Church of Scotland, the Very Rev Dr J. C. Russell. Two other services followed that day and collections totalled £71.13*s*. In 1957 the Rodger Memorial Church (formerly the UF Church) linked with the Established Church, and ten years later the union of the churches was formalised under the name of Annbank Church. Sinking of the church's foundations occurred in the 1960s as a result of mine workings, and the NCB contributed towards the cost of rebuilding part of the structure. James McLaughlin was organist of the church for 49 years, and James Brown MP was an elder for many years. Today there are few changes to the scene depicted here, although the road has been realigned and there is a car park to the left where a recreation club once stood. This became the church hall after suitable conversion. On rising ground to the right of the church is the cemetery, while beyond it is the housing development around Church Drive.

James Brown was born in 1862 in Whitletts, then a hamlet on the road out of Ayr. The son of a weaver, his family moved to Annbank soon after his birth, marking the start of his lifelong connection with the village. He began his education at the village school, leaving, aged twelve, to work in the coal pits. From being a trapper boy (opening and closing the door for pit ponies which hauled hutches), he became a coupler (like a guard on the trains of hutches), then a pony driver before arriving at the coal face at fourteen. Four years later he was a proper miner. He became active in the Ayrshire Miners' Union and at 33 was local president. By 1908 he was general secretary of the National Union of Scottish Mineworkers for the County of Ayr. Just before the First World War the government appointed a Royal Commission on Housing in Scotland. James Brown and Thomas McKerrell, agents for the Ayrshire Miners' Union, submitted a report on the Ayrshire miners' rows of the time. This remains a standard reference work on conditions in miners' homes then (a facsimile edition was produced by the Ayrshire Archaeological and Natural History Society in 1979). After a couple of unsuccessful attempts at standing for Parliament as a Liberal, he won the South Ayrshire seat as the Labour candidate in 1918. Except for a brief period in the early 1930s he held this seat until his death, aged 76, in 1939. A deeply religious man, he was both a church elder and involved with the local Sunday school, and was three times Lord High Commissioner to the General Assembly of the Church of Scotland. A memorial to James Brown was unveiled in June 1954 close to where he had lived with his wife, firstly at No. 56 Annbank, a two-room and kitchen house in a miners' row, then later in a county council house. Those involved in the ceremony included the Lord Lieutenant of Ayrshire, Commander G. H. Hughes-Onslow, the Rev G. A. Johnston, Rev J. Younger Thomson and Rev W. H. Whalley. His name lives on in Ayr where one of the main streets in Whitletts was named James Brown Avenue (known locally as 'Jaba') and of course in Annbank there is Brown's Crescent.

Hugh Dunlop was a familiar figure around Annbank and Mossblown in the early 1900s, carting coal from local pits to miners' houses in the area. Known as 'Bush' (pronounced as in 'lush'), he kept his horse in a field behind Dan Lesley's chip shop in Annbank's Goodwin Drive. Not surprisingly this became known as Bush's Field.

Gilchrist's the bakers of High Street, Ayr, make a delivery of their 'Gold Medal Bread' to Annbank in the early 1920s using their recently acquired van. The village later had its own baker's, Robert Smillie & Son, which originated in Goodwin Drive before moving to Braefoot.

Annbank House was once known as Privick House. The theory put forward on page 12 as to the origin of the name 'Privick' is compounded here, as there was once an orchard to the south of the house which in 1884 is described as containing 'some fine old pear trees'. The name of the house was supposedly changed to Annbank as a compliment to Lady Ann Montgomery, who married the Laird of Privick and Enterkine. Standing in a prominent position high above the River Ayr, the house had fine views upstream, down and across the river. The building dated back to the early part of the eighteenth century and was extended at various times. In the latter part of the nineteenth century it belonged to the coalmaster James Clarke who moved there with his family from Whitburn in West Lothian to manage the local pits of George Taylor & Co. In the early years of the twentieth century the family moved to Afton Lodge, and Annbank House had various owners thereafter, before becoming a hotel in the 1950s. The local pipe band used to play on the lawn in front of the house on Sunday afternoons. At the back, a conservatory provided stunning views over the river. Owing to erosion of the banking, the building became unsafe, and after lying empty for a time and deteriorating it was demolished around 1967–8 and literally bulldozed over the bank.

The River Ayr, seen below where Annbank House stood high above the natural rock weir, with the start of the mill lade on the north (left) bank. Two sluices controlled the water-flow along the lade, which was about eleven feet wide and led to Privick Mill, approximately a quarter of a mile away. The stretch of river from here past Privick Mill to the Old Ha' (page 16) is considered by many to be the most picturesque along its entire length. It was popular for a variety of activities including swimming and fishing, the salmon here reputedly being particularly good. There are numerous pools of varying depths, many with their own local names. The area pictured with its deep pool was known as the Dam; then there was the Garden Pool, followed by the Mill Pool, and further on the Old Ha' Pool, reputed to be the deepest part of the River Ayr at an estimated 55 feet.

Privick Mill. There are various theories as to the derivation of 'Privick', a particularly interesting one suggesting that it comes from the Old English *peru*, pear tree, and *wic*, a dependant farm. The fact that the holm where the mill is situated was once famed for its fine fruit trees lends weight to this theory. The overall impression of the mill is of a mixture of buildings, constructed, altered and added to at different times. Just when it originated is uncertain. There were essentially two mills situated end-on to the river and connected to each other; one was for flour, the other oatmeal. Each had a separate waterwheel, about four feet wide and fifteen feet in diameter, with the discharge water going straight into the river in the case of the flour mill, and via a mill race from the grain mill. The flour mill, built around 1860, had a fairly short existence due to changes in processes. After milling ceased in the mid-1930s the site was taken over by Robert Gilchrist, a native of Lanark, who developed a nursery there growing fruit, vegetables and flowers, both outside and protected. Produce was sold to local shops and further afield, and also sent to the Glasgow Fruit Market. In the half-acre of glasshouses tomatoes, cucumbers, lettuce, chrysanthemums and other cut flowers were grown, while in the open the cropping included potatoes, vegetables and soft fruit – strawberries, raspberries and currants. Many local folk were employed on the nursery, mostly part-time, and particularly children at berry-picking time. It passed to Mr Gilchrist's son, Cranston, and closed in the early 1980s. Little remains of the nursery buildings, the most prominent feature being the chimney stack. An extra section at the top of the 'lum' was added to disperse its smoke when the Whitehill housing was developed, and can still be seen. This view of the mill dates from around 1930. In the right background is Gadgirth House (page 16), with the river running between them. The miller's house, now a private residence, is in the centre. A reminder of the past can be found at the top of the brae, off Privick Mill Road, where, built into the entrance walls to a house are a pair of millstones.

The Gadgirth Bridge pictured here was built by Cameron Richmond in 1879 and replaced the original narrow stone bridge. It is recorded that a stone on one of the southern piers carries the message 'I was built by Mr John Stell (sic) of Gadgirth in 1768'. John Steele, minister of Stair Parish, had inherited Gadgirth Estate from his wife, and prior to his intervention it is likely that the river was crossed by a ford. He died at the age of 93 after 69 years as a minister. The arches of the original bridge were removed and replaced by the iron girder top seen here, with the present plate girder bridge succeeding this in 1909. Just visible on the north bank is the building known as Bulloch's Cottage, now no longer. The bridge marks the boundary between Tarbolton Parish on the north bank and Coylton Parish (south bank).

The row of thatched houses opposite, known as Gadgirth Holm, was built by the Rev John Steele in 1769. Its occupants were mostly miners, there being numerous pits in the area. Between 1798 and 1878 there were eight pits on the Gadgirth Estate alone, and the area became known as the 'Black Neuk' as a result. The row was demolished in 1904 and the cottages illustrated above were built on its site in 1906. Designed in the Arts & Crafts style, they still stand almost 100 years on, although they have been somewhat updated with modernised windows on the ground floor and upper conversions featuring dormers.

This impressive mansion was built in 1808 on the site of a previous building known as Gadgirth Castle, which in turn is believed to have replaced an earlier castle, traces of which are to be seen about three-quarters of a mile downstream and known as Old Ha'. The estate of Gadgirth thus has a long history. It has been suggested that the name derives from the Anglo-Saxon *gad*, a land measure of varying length, and *garth*, enclosed. In 1359 reference is made by the Sheriff of Ayr to the 'Lands of Gadgard'. From around that time the owners were a family known later as Chalmers, but originally as de Camera. The early version of the castle was replaced in the fifteenth century by a structure in a spectacular setting on a promontory overlooking the River Ayr. In 1556 John Knox, the reformer, visited the castle to preach and celebrate communion, the Chalmers at that time being a friend of Knox and supporters of the Reformation. It is reputed that Mary, Queen of Scots, spent the night there (but that has been said of many places!). There was a downturn in the estate's fortunes in the early eighteenth century, and on the death of the last male Chalmers it passed to his eldest sister, who married the minister of Stair Parish, John Steele. He was responsible for many improvements including building a bridge and the original Gadgirth Holm cottages. Gadgirth passed to Rev Steele's daughter by a second marriage and eventually reached Lieutenant Colonel Joseph Burnett, who in the course of trying to improve the old castle only succeeded in having it demolished, replacing it with this mansion house on the same site in 1808. His son, John Joseph Burnett, carried out many improvements on the estate and he in turn was succeeded by his brother, General Francis Claude Burnett. The estate then passed through a series of owners, during which time the house was altered considerably, including modifications in 1903 by the Glasgow firm of architects, Honeyman, Keppie & Mackintosh (Keppie resided in Prestwick and Charles Rennie Mackintosh's name needs no explanation).

The gardens were extensive and varied with glasshouses, herbaceous borders, informal walks and this fine parterre. In 1949 Gadgirth House went out of private hands with Ayr County Council purchasing it at a public auction for £4,300 – a figure described by a council official as 'cheap at the price'! A children's welfare committee of the council had shortly before decided to acquire a home for 'orphaned, deserted and separated children'. Gadgirth fitted the bill and after suitable repairs and modifications it was officially opened in June 1953 as a residence for around two-dozen Ayrshire school-age children who had come under council care. The children's home provided a valuable service for fifteen years, although misbehaving local children were often warned by their parents that they would be put in the home. Its upkeep became too great with necessary structural repairs and it finally closed on 30 June 1968. Not long afterwards it was demolished.

Although this postcard is captioned 'The Bridge, Gadgirth', it is not to be confused with Gadgirth Bridge which carries the main road to Coylton over the River Ayr. Instead this structure stood within Gadgirth Estate, carrying a road to the mansion from a gatehouse over a deep chasm.

The estate of Enterkine dates back to the early part of the seventeenth century when it was in the hands of one of the oldest families in the area, the Dunbars. It passed to a branch of the Cunninghames of Caprington in the mid-seventeenth century. When William Cunninghame came of age in 1788 he inherited the estates of Annbank and Enterkine from his grandfather, the mansion houses of each being in a semi-ruinous state. He organised a memorable fete, inviting the wealthy landlords and aristocracy of Ayrshire to it. While the purpose of the event was supposedly to introduce himself to the nobility, it was assumed by many that it was actually a means of canvassing support to become a member of parliament, the current house being due to be dissolved soon after. Robert Burns wrote a semi-political song entitled *The Fete Champetre* in which he pointed out how 'wine' and 'coin' were used to buy votes at that time and the sham of aristocratic politics. It contains the lines: 'Annbank, wha guess'd the ladies taste, He gies a Fete Champetre'. This is believed to be the only time that Annbank appears in the bard's works, albeit referring to a person rather than the place. While Cunninghame was not chosen as a candidate, it is widely believed that he did not allow his name to go forward in the end. There is some doubt as to exactly where the 'fete champetre' took place. While it has been suggested that it was on a holm to the south of Annbank House, it seems more likely to have been on the holm on the north bank of the river immediately below the original Enterkine House. Whatever the venue the fete seems to have lasted three days with the guests feasting, dancing and whatever else, the proceedings coming to an abrupt end with a tremendous thunderstorm. Cunninghame later married Catherine Stewart, daughter of Burns' patron Mrs Stewart of Stair and Afton, and sold the latter 40 acres of land on which Afton Lodge was built. His son succeeded him and in 1830 the estate was sold to John Bell of Blackhouse, Ayr. By 1879 Bell owned 2,256 acres of land in the surrounding area. He died in 1914 aged 73 years, leaving it to his son. The original Enterkine House was replaced by the late-Georgian mansion shown here. It was however considered too large and expensive to run and was demolished to be replaced by the present mansion, built in 1939. For many years this was owned by the Hon Alan McKay, and is now Enterkine Country House Hotel. In California there is reputed to be a house built to the identical design of Enterkine, and, on the American theme, Lee Trevino stayed on Enterkine Estate when appearing at the Open at Troon in the 1970s.

Annbank brickworks, if one studies early maps, were at different locations at different times. Around 1900 they were at Springs, but the site where they are most likely to be remembered is close to Annbank Road, towards Mossblown from Weston Toll, and adjacent to the railway line. The works belonged to Bairds & Dalmellington prior to takeover by the NCB, and were in production from the 1920s until closure in the sixties, after which they were demolished. Fireclay from bands in the coal measures in the nearby Enterkine pits was used to make the bricks, and at the works' peak about 30,000 were produced each day. They were reputed to be bigger than a standard modern brick. This picture shows Annbank brickworks looking towards Mossblown. The aerial track in the foreground connected with Enterkine Colliery close by. Beyond the works is part of Muirburn Farm and the Established Church, with the main road snaking down towards Mossblown.

Although captioned 'Station Road', this postcard actually shows Annbank Road around 1920. Overlooking the field of 'stooks' is the school, opened in 1903, beside which, conveniently situated, is the schoolmaster's house. The school is still recognisable and the 'heedie's' house is now a private dwelling (albeit occupied by a former headmaster of the school!). Beyond the cottages is St Ann's. Built in 1898 as a chapel/school, it doubled as the latter until a separate primary school was built in 1931. The Parish of St Ann's was established in 1898, a daughter parish of St Margaret's, Ayr. Prior to this the Roman Catholic congregation had worshipped first in the old school at Weston and then in a newly erected iron chapel at the end of Brocklehill Avenue. The name of John Cameron was associated with St Ann's for a period of almost 50 years: on the occasion of his being made a Canon of the Diocese of Galloway in 1938 he was described as having taken St Ann's to become 'one of the finest churches in the diocese'. He continued to serve at Mossblown until his death in 1947. Next to the church is the police house, and just visible in the background are the rows of Drumley.

Sitting on the corner of Station Road and Annbank Road, Mossblown, in this early 1920s view, is the private house of Lochnorris which doubled as the village post office. Built in 1906, Lochnorris was owned by Thomas Murray, a joiner, when this postcard was produced. The post office replaced an earlier one operated in the former Bogend tollhouse. Around 1926 William Paton and his wife Janet took over and were still there in the 1940s. The car outside the post office is a Model T Ford – where today can you park at the post office and not be on a double yellow line? Just up Station Road is the UF Church manse which at this time would have been occupied by Rev Edward Brown.

Annbank Station was opened on 1 September 1870 by the Glasgow & South Western Railway, initially serving the Ayr to Mauchline route, but also from June 1872 the Cronberry line, referred to as the 'A&C' (Ayr and Cumnock). The Ayrshire lines were initially planned for mineral traffic, passengers being a secondary consideration, and as a result stations like Annbank were frequently a considerable distance from the village whose names they bore, Tarbolton being another good example locally. In time the station was well-used by passengers, probably most extensively during the halcyon days of Annbank United, when football specials were frequent, transporting hundreds of fans to venues as varied as Aberdeen and Armadale. The station had four platforms, two for the Cumnock line and two for the Mauchline line, with its main buildings on the Ayr-bound platform. This picture, which shows the ticket office, waiting room and goods depot, dates from the late 1920s, by which time the station was under the control of the LMS (London, Midland & Scottish) Railway, as can be seen on the board. Standing on the platform, are, from right to left: William Watson (signalman); Willie Bruce (porter); D. McAlpine; and an unknown gentleman. George Downie was stationmaster at this time. Railway employees lived in company houses (since demolished) in Station Road, and included signalmen, pointsmen, surfacemen and porters. The station closed to passengers on 10 September 1951 and for freight on 5 July 1964.

Bogend Toll, otherwise known as the 'Penny Toll', was at the crossroads of the turnpike road from Monkton to Gadgirth Bridge and on to Coylton, and the road from Ayr to Mauchline. Pictured here, looking towards Ayr, are the tollhouse on the left and Stockbridge Cottage on the right. Today this is the site of staggered crossroads on the Ayr to Mauchline road, with the turning to Sandyford on the right and to Annbank on the left. Few people who travel through here will be aware of the tragedy which occurred in the vicinity over 120 years ago. Back in September 1877 the proprietor of Enterkine Sawmills, James McQuater, and his family occupied both cottage and tollhouse, together with two of Mr McQuater's employees who lodged with them. His mother-in-law, Margaret Taylor, was the toll-keeper. Early one day Eliza McQuater, the thirteen-year-old daughter of the sawmiller, failed to return from going to fetch cows from a nearby field. She was found with severe injuries, a meat cleaver nearby, and despite the efforts of the local (legendary) Dr McGill, died the next day. Suspicion fell on John Bell, a sawmill employee who lodged with Mrs Taylor and who had disappeared from the house. Next day he was found in nearby bushes, apparently having attempted to cut his throat. When it was discovered he was still alive, he was loaded on to a special engine and van at Annbank Station and taken to Ayr railway station and thence to hospital. He survived and was promptly charged with Eliza's murder. Just three weeks later her father died. At his trial in Ayr the following March, Bell's plea of 'guilty but insane' was not accepted and he was found guilty of murder and sentenced to be hanged at Ayr prison. On hearing the verdict he addressed the court, explaining how he had 'gone astray': 'Reading of novels and drinking whisky was my first start in crime . . . my mind was carried away by reading novels' (the trial reports didn't reveal the titles of the offending books!). Nine days before his execution date, Bell was informed by the Home Secretary that the Queen had commanded that his sentence be respited. He remained in prison for seventeen years before being released on medical grounds.

This view of the Penny Toll looking towards Annbank dates from the early years of the last century. The former Bogend tollhouse doubled as the village post office, prior to its removal to Lochnorris (page 21), and the post box is visible to the right of the door. Mr and Mrs John Laurie followed the octogenarian toll-keeper Margaret Taylor into the property in May 1883, one week before the toll bar system ceased. They lived there and at Stockbridge Cottage on the opposite side of the Ayr road for over 30 years, with Mr Laurie working at the local pit for 61 years. Mrs Laurie (the name was pronounced 'Lowrie', as in 'matchstick men') was well-known for making dolls in which she used her own hair. There is an interesting story as to where she may have learned this activity, but not the space here to tell it! The couple celebrated their golden wedding anniversary in 1914 with a 'do' in the Co-operative Hall. The building on the left corner was originally a block of four houses for Co-op staff and remained as housing for much of the twentieth century. In recent years there have been changes, with a hairdresser, a baker and a general store setting up business there, while at the time of writing it is in use as the Fourways lounge bar. Just up Annbank road is the Co-operative premises comprising shops and bakery on the ground floor with houses above.

The Co-op dominated the shopping scene in Mossblown for the greater part of the twentieth century. Initially the Annbank Co-operative Society, it amalgamated with the KECS (Kilmarnock Equitable Co-operative Society) in 1910. Above the shop there was housing, and at the back stables and a cartshed, later converted to garaging and stores. To the rear, also, was the hall. Many a wedding reception, after-the-funeral tea, presentation – in fact, 'do' of any sort – was held in the Co-operative Hall. On Saturday 22 March 1958 there was great excitement when fire gutted the Co-op, with the bakery, back shop, hall and two houses badly affected. The fire started when a lorry collecting empties was reversing at the rear of the building. It knocked over a drum of petrol which spilled over a bunker of coal. An inspection lamp nearby fused and soon flames swept through the rear shop and bakehouse. Damage estimated at £20,000 was caused, but fortunately the front shop was only slightly affected by water and was able to open for business the following Monday. The 'store' (as it was known) eventually closed for business in the 1960s, and the premises – now minus an upper storey – have been used for various purposes since, including a garage. They are currently occupied by a tile and bathroom showroom. In this picture Maggie Scott (the clerk) is joined by colleagues Willie McIntyre and Andrew Ferguson, amongst others.

The United Free Church was formerly a mission station of Tarbolton Free Church. Alexander Rodger, born and educated in Glasgow, became ordained preacher at Tarbolton St John's in 1893–96 and was inducted at Tarbolton in 1896. He was called to Aberdeen Union in 1904, followed by Edinburgh Coats Memorial in 1906, before returning to Annbank in 1914 and taking over from George Swanson. Following Rev Rodger's retiral in 1917 the church became known as the Rodger Memorial Church, and was subsequently served by Edward Brown, Andrew Strachan, George Christie and James Byers. It linked with Annbank Old in 1957 and became united with it ten years later. At the time of writing the building was being used as Annbank Church hall. The house to the left of the church is Park View, while on the far left is the Co-op building. On the opposite side of the road was the 'Meadow', a badly drained area liable to flooding and used as a refuse coup. In winter when it flooded and froze it became a makeshift skating rink.

The party standing in the roadway outside the post office look to be more interested in the camera than going for a hurl in the almost new 'Baby' Austin 7, registered in 1928. Beyond the Free Church manse and Roselee Cottage are the then recently built two-storey blocks which housed mine managers.

A quiet day looking up Annbank Road in the late 1920s. Third on the left is the police station, where local bobby Constable John Hyslop lived around this time. The prominent building next door is the chapel and schoolhouse of St Ann's, built in 1898. A little further on is the cottage known as Beau Sejour, home of Miss J. Thomson, district nurse in the area for over 22 years before retiring in 1943. Many of the cottages along Annbank Road had delightful names, including Elderlee, Florence Court, Laurelbank, Cloverlea, Guillaume, and Laverock, to name but a few. In the distance is the Clarke Memorial Hall. This was gifted to the community by James A. Clarke of Afton Lodge, a local coalmaster, and was built on a site provided free of charge by Major Julian Oswald to a design by Ayr architect Allan Stevenson. It could seat about 450 and there was also a lesser hall and appropriate 'retiring rooms'. The basement housed a kitchen, while above the front was a four-apartment caretaker's house.

The opening ceremony for the Clarke Memorial Hall was held on Friday 5 February 1926, James Clarke presenting it to the community and James Brown MP acknowledging the gift. Miss Clarke of Afton Lodge and Mrs Davidson of Templehurst donated a piano. This was soon put into use in a concert which was followed by a dance. Amongst the delights of the soiree were a ventriloquist, Mr Bob Johnstone; Miss Meta Paton, who gave a reading entitled 'The Bapteezement o' the Bairn'; Miss Norah Vance, a contralto, with 'Home Sweet Home'; Mr Sam G. Shimmons, a baritone, with 'Comrades of Yesterday'; while Mr Robert R. Welsh, a violinist, provided 'Souvenir de Sorrento'. Rae Welsh, as he became known, went on to become a violin teacher of renown throughout Ayrshire and beyond. His string orchestra performed at events across the land and in 1951 played at the Festival of Britain in London. The former Clarke Memorial Hall is now the community centre, as proclaimed on the outside by a South Ayrshire Council board reading 'Mossblown and Drumly (sic) Community Centre' (interesting to see this spelling on a building right next to the school!). The caretaker of the hall in the mid-1930s was Robert Holland, who lived on the premises. In the mid-1940s Mrs Doolan lived in the first of the houses next to the hall. She worked at the school and also had a wee shop selling sweeties and 'ginger'.

Around the middle of the nineteenth century the Cunninghames of Enterkine sold their estate to John Bell. He had made his fortune in the West Indies, and on realising that there were large coal reserves under his new property he promptly leased the mineral rights to George Taylor & Co. of the Ayr Coal Company. The coal company then took over the running of Weston School, collecting contributions from the miners to pay for its upkeep, but in 1873, as a result of the Education (Scotland) Act, responsibility for the school transferred to Tarbolton School Board. By this time the population around Annbank Station was growing with the building of the miners' rows at Mossblown and Drumley, and after much wrangling it was decided to built a new school on a site near Annbank Station, provided by the owner of the Auchencruive estate, Richard Oswald (who owned 11,004 acres in Ayrshire in 1874). This school would serve the older children from Annbank (infants would remain at the original school) and all the children from the Annbank Station area. The new school was officially opened on 30 September 1903, and its facade remains similar today, although over the past 100 years there have been many extensions and other alterations. In its centenary year Annbank Primary School produced a very readable history of the school.

A striking view of Mossblown Pit (Auchencruive 1, 2 and 3). This, the last major pit in the area, closed at the end of December 1960 after 60 years of production. Its first two shafts were sunk in 1898, with a third added in 1910. By 1938, 725 men were employed below ground and 260 at the surface. The owners at the time were Bairds & Dalmellington, with D. McKinnon and J. Bell the manager and under-manager respectively. Two years later peak production of 1,700 tons of coal per day was reached. At the time of nationalisation in 1947 the decision was made to run down Mossblown when Killoch came into production. Gradually manpower was reduced, the workforce being transferred to Killoch Colliery and other pits in the area, although even approaching the end Mossblown's output was 200 tons per day. Concentrated to the left of the road to Sandyford are the pit-head operations, while on the other side of the road are the colliery baths, which were built around 1933. The single-track mineral railway running alongside the sidings opened in 1892 from the newly created Mossblown Junction and joined the Ayr to Glasgow line at Monkton. At the top left of the picture is Mainshaw Farm, now demolished, while running from left to right just below it is the trackbed of a former railway line to nearby Tofts Pit. The twin chimney stacks were demolished in July 1962 and most of the site cleared. The baths building remains, although in a much-altered state, it having been converted into a meat processing plant (formerly known as Sandyford Foods) which supplies major supermarket chains.

Miners' housing at Mossblown was built by the company to the west of the Mauchline road and on either side of the railway line, with a total of 179 houses constructed in five rows in a somewhat irregular fashion between 1895 and 1911. These did not have official names, and to begin with were simply known as 1–179 Mossblown. The older part of Mossblown, dating from around 1896 and located on the north side of the railway, comprised two rows of two-apartment brick-built houses, the kitchens of which measured 15 feet by 13½ and the rooms 13½ by 10½ feet. A wash-house was shared by every six tenants, and a dry closet by every three. The first row of 28 houses became known as the 'Pole Raw', supposedly because of the number of Lithuanian and Polish workers who lived there, brought in by the mine company (today Arcan Avenue lies roughly on the site of Pole Raw). The other row, imaginatively called 'Lang Raw', contained 69 houses which were identical in layout to those in Pole Raw. Today Hillpark stands on the site of Lang Raw (confusingly it was originally known as Pole Road). This picture shows the eastern end of Lang Raw looking across the Mauchline road towards the railway signal box. Pictured left to right are: D. White (bookie); D. Jackson; _____; Mrs Winslow; Net Aitken; _____; Mrs Sam Hay (Peggy White); Jerry Irvine; and Bert McClelland.

South of the railway a further three rows were built around 1909. Short Raw and Back Raw comprised 32 and 38 two-apartment houses respectively, and stood roughly where today's Barwheys Drive is. The third row, known as 'The Cottages', was made up of twelve three-apartment houses and was demolished in the early 1970s, much later than the other rows. It was replaced by the present bungalow-style housing in Sandyford Road. Despite their houses being larger, tenants of The Cottages still had to share communal facilities, with a wash-house for every six and a water-closet this time for every two. Here The Cottages are seen looking towards Bogend Toll with the road to Annbank in the background. Described in the 1913 report on Ayrshire miners' rows as having 'nice flower plots at the front inside wooden railings', the houses also featured 'a nice lobby and a good sized scullery fitted with a kitchen sink and water tap'.

The road from Ayr is deserted in this 1920s view approaching Bogend Toll. Beyond the shed on the left is Stockbridge Cottage, situated on the corner of the road to Sandyford. The group of boys are in front of The Cottages, which stretch across the picture, while visible through the gap between them is one of the other rows. Eighty years on, the scene has changed completely. Apart from obvious differences in road layout, The Cottages have all gone, some replaced by the housing of Murray Court. The dominating Mossblown Activity Centre now occupies the site to the right.

In immediate post-war Britain there was a desperate housing shortage, and to tackle this almost 150,000 prefabricated houses were built. Mossblown had its own quota of prefabs, which were modern inside, having both a kitchen and bathroom, making them a vast improvement on the old miners' rows. Despite being small and having condensation problems – there was only one fire in the house – the prefabs were generally loved by their occupants and often had well-tended gardens. Those in the picture stood in the area where Drumley Avenue now is, and although originally intended as a short-term solution were not demolished and replaced by 'proper' houses until around 1960. The nearest prefab belonged to Mr Frew, who ran the Gospel Hall in Sandyford Road.

Opened in the mid-1890s, Drumley Pit (Ayr Colliery 1 & 2) was situated between the Mauchline road and the railway line to Mauchline at Southside. It had a comparatively short life, closing prior to nationalisation in 1947. Early in 1928 it ceased production due to a lack of orders, resulting in between 250 and 300 men being idle for almost a year before it resumed operations in March 1929. Drumley was connected underground with Enterkine Nos. 9 & 10, and served as an escape route and ventilation upcast. Here the proximity of the rows to the 'pitheid' can be clearly seen, the single-storey rows nearest the camera with their back-to-back two-storey neighbours beyond. An interesting selection of wagons are in the sidings in the foreground, with the Caledonian, North British and Glasgow & South Western Railways represented.

The owners of Drumley Pit built 36 houses (all of which had two apartments) in two rows for the workers at Drumley. One row of twenty houses, built back to back, comprised two-storey dwellings with the kitchen below and the room above. There was a second row of sixteen single-storey houses. Each house in both rows had a dry closet, and wash-houses were shared between five families. Water was obtained from pumps situated in front of the rows. This sketch by local resident Hugh McIntyre shows part of the single-storey row with wash-house and drying area.

Taken from the bridge on the Ayr to Mauchline road in Mossblown on a snowy day, this view is dominated by the bing which was a local landmark for many years. Annbank Station is prominent, with its four platforms connected by a footbridge. The line curving to the right past the station buildings meandered through stations at Trabboch and Drongan, by Belston Junction and Ochiltree and on to Cumnock. That straight on led by way of Tarbolton Station to Mauchline, where it joined the main line. In the left background is Drumley Pit, actively worked for 50 years, with its tall chimney and pithead paraphernalia. A gangway leads from the pithead over the railway to the bing with its elevator to the top. The white building just visible behind the wall (centre left), is part of the farm buildings of Whiskeyhall (or Whiskeyha'), in the Thom family for many years. The pit closed in the 1950s and the bing, a favourite with children for scrambling up and sliding down, was flattened and landscaped, the spoil being used in the construction of a runway extension at Prestwick Airport and the Ayr bypass.

This group of miners at Drumley Colliery posed for the camera around 1914. Of the 34 individuals here, how many can you name? To help, for starters, there is William Monaghan, Joe Livingstone, Jock Dunlop, Bog Agnew, Tom Hay, the McGaffney brothers, Tom Purdie, Dan Murphy and Gibby Kerr.

The Miners Accidents (Rescue & Aid) Act of 1910 required all mines to provide and maintain rescue equipment and to train employees in both rescue and first aid procedures. The Mines Rescue Brigade were specially trained men who, in the event of an emergency, were called out to organise and carry out rescue work. This group at a practice session illustrates the cumbersome apparatus they carried, especially the headgear. The men are wearing WEG breathing apparatus (named after the inventor, W. E. Garforth) which mixed purified exhaled air with oxygen. First aid classes were held regularly in the community centre.

On 1 March 1912 miners across the country went on strike for a minimum wage. The action lasted until mid-April when the Miners' Federation of Great Britain brought it to an end, but not before the strikers had caused a major coup, uniting as one force for the first time and making this the first national coal strike. Over the years more strikes were to follow, bringing in their wake hardship to many. During such times everyone helped his neighbour and fund-raising activities were many and varied. Drumley was one of the pits involved in the 1912 strike, and this motley crew formed a 'band' which provided entertainment and brought in funds. With their array of 'instruments' including squeeze boxes, comb and paper, flute, biscuit tin drum and horseshoe are, left to right:
Back row: P. Price; Jas Dunlop; P. Price; G. Dunlop; R. Frew; T. Purdie; Jas McCready; B. Price; W. Hainey
Centre (either side of bass drum): Jas Riddick; R. Mossie
Front row: Alex Martin; Ter. McMillan; Jas Hart; W. McCarroll; J. Ferguson

In the aftermath of the demolition of the Drumley 'lum' in October 1952 a mixed group examine the demolisher's handiwork. On this occasion Fred Dibnah did not attend! Wearing raincoat and hat is John Davy from the NCB, while the capless figure to the left is Jim Bell of Drumley. With her young daughter, Betty, is Isabel McDonald accompanied by son Alex. On the extreme right in the foreground, watching the camera, is John Harrigan, with John Mathison alongside.

Annbank Junction signal box (formerly known as Annbank No. 1 and renamed in 1966 on the closure of Annbank No. 2 box) is seen here in May 1982, less than three years before it closed, when the Mauchline line (disappearing to the left) was put in a reserved state and effectively shut. From the box's elevated position at the top of a cutting, the signalman could look out over the bridge carrying the Ayr–Mauchline road and see trains approaching from Ayr. However, the elevation meant that he had a long, exposed descent to track level, and that signal wires and point rods had to be taken down the embankment by a series of pulley wheels and cranks. In the foreground on either side of the crossing are the wooden platforms where tokens could be exchanged for single line working. Beyond the box are houses in Southside Avenue, built where Drumley Colliery had stood.

There are many intriguing features about Neilshill House, a villa built of red sandstone *c*.1880. While the building itself is Italianate in design, the 'keyhole' windows are not. There is a Moorish flavour about the house, both inside and out, with arched doorways, painted glass panels and a 'fountain-hall' of eight sides. The house has now been converted into flats. A lodge of similar design was nicknamed 'Keyhole Kate's' by local youngsters.

Situated a little to the north of Templehouse is Afton Lodge, built around 1790 for Mrs Catherine Stewart of Afton, who previously lived at Stair House. Mrs Stewart was one of Robert Burns' earliest patrons and in 1791 he sent her a collection of hitherto unpublished works which included *Tam o' Shanter* and *Sweet Afton*. This collection is known as the Afton Manuscript. It was thought for a time that the song *Sweet Afton* was written for Mrs Stewart and that the 'Afton' referred to was a stream near to Afton Lodge. Burns himself however made it clear that he was referring to the River Afton at New Cumnock. The house clearly got its name from Mrs Stewart's past, she being a daughter of James Gordon of Afton. Various alterations were carried out to the building in the first quarter of the twentieth century to plans by the prolific local architect Allan Stevenson. It is quite similar in appearance to Drumley House.

This postcard, sent in 1904, bears the message 'Here is the view of the front of our house. Love from May Watson'. May was the wife of Peter Watson, cashier of George Taylor & Co., coalmasters, who were tenants of the property, the owner being James A. Clarke. Readers may recognise the building as Templehouse, the mansion which became the care home of today, yet on maps and other documents from Victorian times it is named High Drumley, 'Templehouse' being applied to a small cottage a few hundred yards away still standing today on the opposite side of the Mauchline road. The name changes present an interesting story. The mansion dates from the latter half of the nineteenth century and maps, census records and valuation rolls clearly have it named as High Drumley. In the meantime the cottage was named Templehouse, being part of the estate of Townhead of Drumley, and was occupied variously by miners and ploughmen. In his *History of the Counties of Ayr and Wigton* (1863), Paterson refers to 'Temple-house' as being the residence of Marion Sawers in 1591 and the probability that there had been 'a place of worship at or near Temple-house'. By 1918 High Drumley had become known as 'Templehurst', and it remained that until around 1928 when it changed to Templehouse. Just how these changes came about is unclear, particularly when in the 1929–30 valuation roll there is the situation of practically adjacent entries for the mansion Templehouse and the cottage Templehouse! Once owned by James Clarke of Afton Lodge, the mansion had several different owners before being run as a hotel for a short time in the 1980s. In 1988 it was converted into a nursing home, having undergone considerable alterations and additions. At the time of writing it is known as Temple House Care Home, and its residents enjoy a rural setting with fine views over the countryside to the rear of the building.

The hamlet of Burnbrae was situated on the road from Weston to Gadgirth Holm, just west of Crawfordston Farm. In the mid-nineteenth century Burnbrae was made up of nineteen houses built of lime-washed stone with thatched roofs (later slated). At the start of the twentieth century there were three rows known as Wilson's Row, Cree's Row and Martin's Row – undoubtedly named after families who lived there. This well-dressed group posed for the photographer at a time when at least one of the rows was still thatched. They are four generations of the Cree family.

It has been suggested that the hamlet of Burnbrae could date back to the eighteenth century and that some of the houses were built of boulders taken from the bed of the nearby River Ayr. The story goes that in 1901 a photographic exhibition was held in Glasgow and a photograph of Burnbrae with Enterkine Viaduct in the background won the top award. No doubt this image was later reproduced in postcard form, as seen here. A china manufacturing company, Grafton, put this picture on one of its products, a tea-set, at least one of which is still in existence. Burnbrae's occupants were mostly miners originally working in the many small, shallow pits in the area, and later in the Ayr Colliery Company's numerous local pits. Towards the end of 1928 the cottages were demolished, their former occupants having left and found new housing elsewhere. In this view of Burnbrae, Crawfordston Farm can be seen in the middle distance, with beyond it the fifteen-span Enterkine Viaduct carrying the single-track A&C railway. Built in 1872, the shallow plate girder structure on masonry pillars is about 91 feet above the River Ayr at its highest point. At either end of the viaduct – known to railwaymen as No. 9 – there is an oval stone with the name of the builder and date of opening.

This picture of Burnbrae appeared in the *Manchester Guardian* (yes, that's correct!) of 13 December 1928, captioned 'Old cottages which have stood for more than 200 years being burnt. They are made of stone bound together with clay instead of mortar.'

The hamlet of Craighall stood perched high above the River Ayr at a bend close to, but on the opposite bank from, Tarholm, and near to the Annbank–Coylton road. There were twenty houses in three rows, one facing south, one facing north and the third facing east to the road. Exactly when the houses were built is uncertain, but one theory is that they were originally stabling accommodation, probably dating from the latter half of the eighteenth century: the layout of the three rows would bear this out. At the time of the 1841 census twenty families lived at Craighall. Close by, to the west, was Barrackhall, described in 1884 as 'a row of low thatched cottages near the road where stand some fine old mulberry trees'. Tradition has it that there was at one time a cavalry barracks there – hence the name – and this would tie in with the suggestion above that Craighall had originated as stables. A little further on is Leglen Wood, in which William Wallace is said to have often found a 'silent and safe retreat' while fleeing from the English. Towards the end of 1933 a local newspaper reported that the hamlet was soon to disappear, with only two of the houses remaining occupied and the others being demolished. Former residents found accommodation in Annbank. This picture shows two sides of Craighall's U-shaped layout, with the rows looking rather bleak, their last days being not far off. Barrackhall is to the left in the distance. The nearest row looks over the river towards Tarholm.

Tarholm consisted of two rows of thatched cottages, one on either side of the road, parallel to it but set back from it. One was located roughly where Tarholm Nursery is today, the other where Windyhill Nursery was. This picture shows Mrs Isabella Aitken of Tarholm beside the 'Big Row'.

Looking towards Tarholm from Tarholm Bridge, the row on the left ('Big Row') had its gardens in front, while that on the right ('Wee Row') had gardens to the back. This picture shows the Wee Row. The bridge itself is somewhat unusual with concrete balustrades resting on sandstone piers, and is the third bridge to cross the river here. The story goes that Archibald Cochrane, 9th Earl of Dundonald, made tar here in olden times out of coal mined locally, selling it to the navy, hence the hamlet's name. Certainly, in the late eighteenth century, Cochrane did patent a distillation process yielding tar, lamp black, coke and gas from coal. His inventions were intended to benefit the navy by using tar as a wood preservative for ship's bottoms. Tarholm had a strong community spirit and enjoyed friendly rivalry with nearby Craighall. This could take the form of football at 'Patrick's Park' (an improvised affair), quoiting at the 'fit o' the Craighall Brae', racing pigeons ('doos'), and garden produce at shows. Families long associated with Tarholm included McCroskie, Fergie, Aitken, Sweden, Curran and Jess.

The hamlet of Woodside was situated on the east side of the Belston to Stair road and south of the A&C railway line. Built to house workers in the nearby collieries, it was owned by various companies including George Taylor & Co. of the Ayr Colliery. Woodside comprised four distinct rows totalling 37 houses, a third of which were two-apartment with very small rooms, with the remaining 25 single-apartment with rooms measuring 15½ by 12½ feet. A large opening between the rows was know as the 'big close'. Brown, on his visit in December 1913, presented a somewhat grim picture. There was a dry closet for every three houses and a wash-house for every six. Understandably 'the womenfolk complained bitterly against the lack of closet accommodation', there being 'no locks on any of the closet doors and some . . . were unspeakably dirty'. The open syvors were seen to be 'sluggish and dirty', although the menfolk took a keen interest in the cultivation of the gardens at the back. The report on Woodside concluded with the poignant comment: 'the people here are of a good type and deserve better accommodation'. It didn't seem to be all bad, as around 1928 the occupiers were given the chance to purchase their homes, as indicated by this document, and all the tenants then became homeowners. Community spirit was high, with open air dancing a feature of village life, the men playing football and quoiting popular too. Woodside stood on the boundary of Coylton and Stair Parishes, although the villagers walked the three miles to Coylton Kirk. With increased transport and buses passing through the village there was inevitably much more contact with the 'outside world', and by 1954 the residents of Woodside had all left and the hamlet was in the hands of the demolishers.

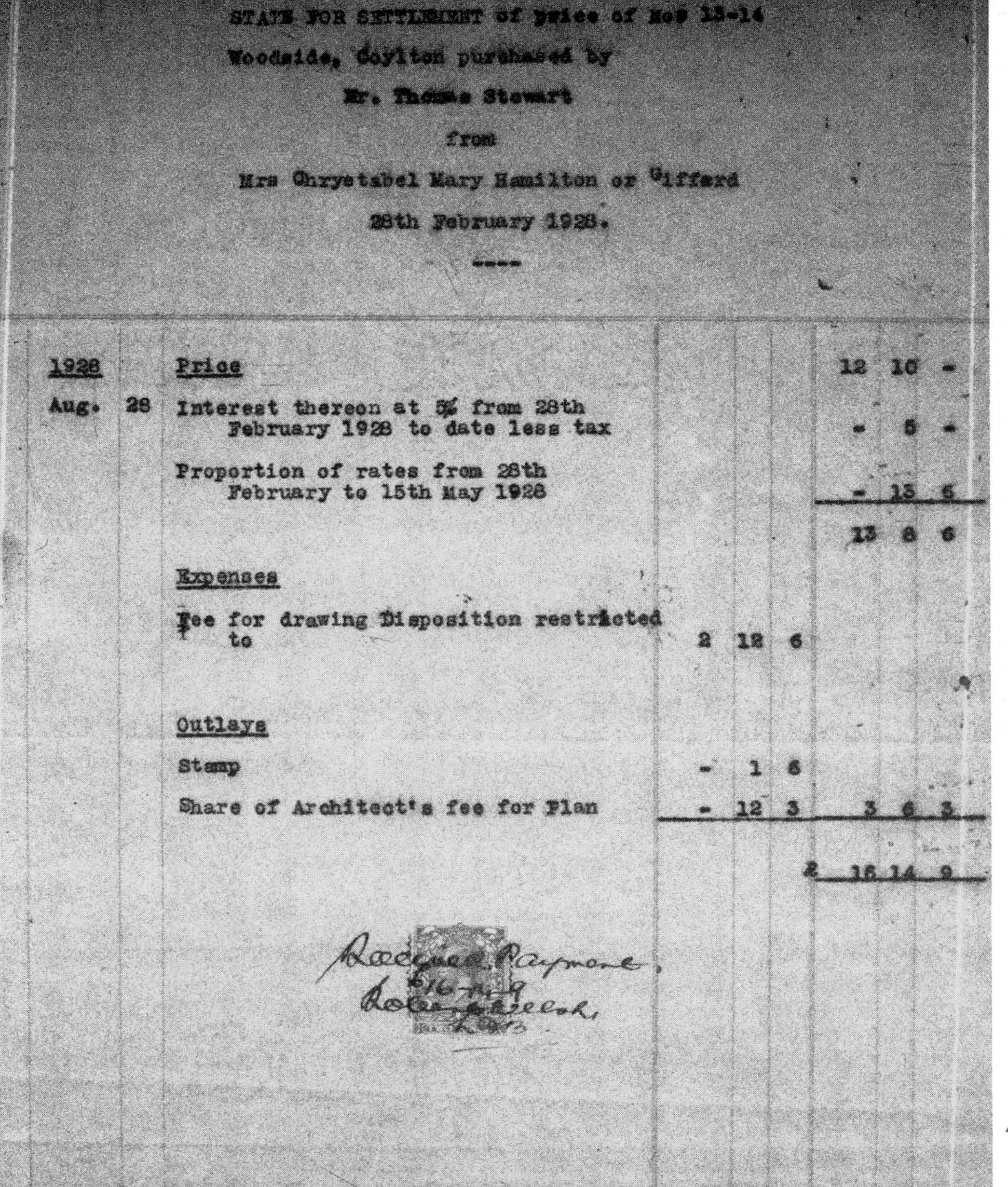

STATE FOR SETTLEMENT of price of Nos 13-14
Woodside, Coylton purchased by
Mr. Thomas Stewart
from
Mrs Chrystabel Mary Hamilton or Gifford
28th February 1928.

1928		Price		12 10 -
Aug.	28	Interest thereon at 5% from 28th February 1928 to date less tax		- 3 -
		Proportion of rates from 28th February to 15th May 1928		- 15 6
				13 8 6
		Expenses		
		Fee for drawing Disposition restricted to	2 12 6	
		Outlays		
		Stamp	- 1 6	
		Share of Architect's fee for Plan	- 12 3	3 6 3
				£ 16 14 9

Early maps of Annbank show a bowling green situated at the bottom of the village behind the reading room and post office, although little is known of the activities of a bowling club in those days. What is certain is that Annbank was affected by the miners' strike in 1921 and Annbank Bowling Club disbanded that year. For seventeen years not a single bowling match took place in the village, but in December 1936 it was decided to form a new club, find a new site and construct a new green – no mean feat. Bairds & Dalmellington provided land at Brocklehill Avenue and gave help with the construction, but it was the village folk themselves who did the grafting. They raised funds through subscriptions, concerts, whist drives and the like, and toiled long and hard to fulfil their dream. This was achieved in June 1938 when Mr R. L. Angus of Ladykirk, chairman of Bairds & Dalmellington, declared the new green, which could accommodate six rinks, open. At that time membership of Annbank Bowling Club was 180, with George Hogg president, Mr A. O. Martin vice-president, and Mr R. Dunlop secretary. This group photograph of club members in 1940 contains many of the individuals who worked so hard to have the new green opened just two years earlier, and includes J. Doolan, several Gourlays, Frank Kerr and Arnold Scott. Since its establishment the club has gone from strength to strength. The women have won, amongst others, the Ayrshire Singles on numerous occasions, Scottish Pairs twice, Scottish Singles twice, British Singles twice and Commonwealth Games Pairs once, and club members have included internationalists Peggy Gourlay, Sarah Gourlay, Annie Leslie, Margaret Scott and Maureen Shimmons. The men's honours include a gold medal at the Commonwealth Games in 1982, Team Gold Medal and Team Bronze in the rinks at Aberdeen in 1984, winning the Ayr Singles twice and the Scottish Singles once. The achievements of their internationalists David Gourlay Snr and David Gourlay Jnr are legendary.

As far back as 1879 the fledgling village of Annbank had a football team. They played at Pebble Park, situated at the end of what became Brocklehill Avenue, close to the river and a disused quarry. The team, known simply as Annbank Football Club, rapidly built up a reputation and in season 1889–90 won the Ayrshire Association Cup, a feat they repeated twice in the next four years. The also won the Charity Cup three times in the same decade. In 1896 they beat East Stirlingshire 3–1 in the first Scottish Qualifying Cup tournament. They became known as the 'White Brigade' on account of their white strip, and until the outbreak of the First World War enjoyed success after success, but it was not to last. After a long history in Ayrshire senior football the club folded in the early 1920s. In the early part of the century there were other local Ayrshire & District Junior League teams whose names didn't always seem to match the brawny players, including Annbank Primrose, Annbank Thistle, Drumley Primrose, Mossblown Strollers and Mossblown Rangers. Juvenile clubs took over the football scene in the 1930s with teams such as Mossblown Toffees (run by 'Toffee' Jock, who had a shop). Annbank United was formed in 1939 and became a member of the Western League. Their first president was William Dunlop with 'Wattie' McLaughlin club secretary. The club soon made its mark, winning the Junior Challenge Cup in the 1940–41 season. In 1949 it moved to New Pebble Park, off Weston Avenue, opening with a game against Auchinleck Talbot on 6 August 1949. Over the years United have won many honours, but regrettably the 'big two' in the Junior game have eluded them. In 1953, playing Vale of Leven at Hampden Park in front of a massive crowd, they were defeated 1–0 in the Scottish Junior Cup final. During the fifties and sixties fans travelled the length and breadth of the country in droves to follow their team, often by special trains from Annbank Station and even on occasion by plane. The club's most successful season was 1987–8 when they won the Blaney Trophy, Kyle & Carrick District Cup, Ayrshire Super Cup and Jackie Scarlett League Cup. Over the years many players have gone on to join the senior ranks – too many to name here.

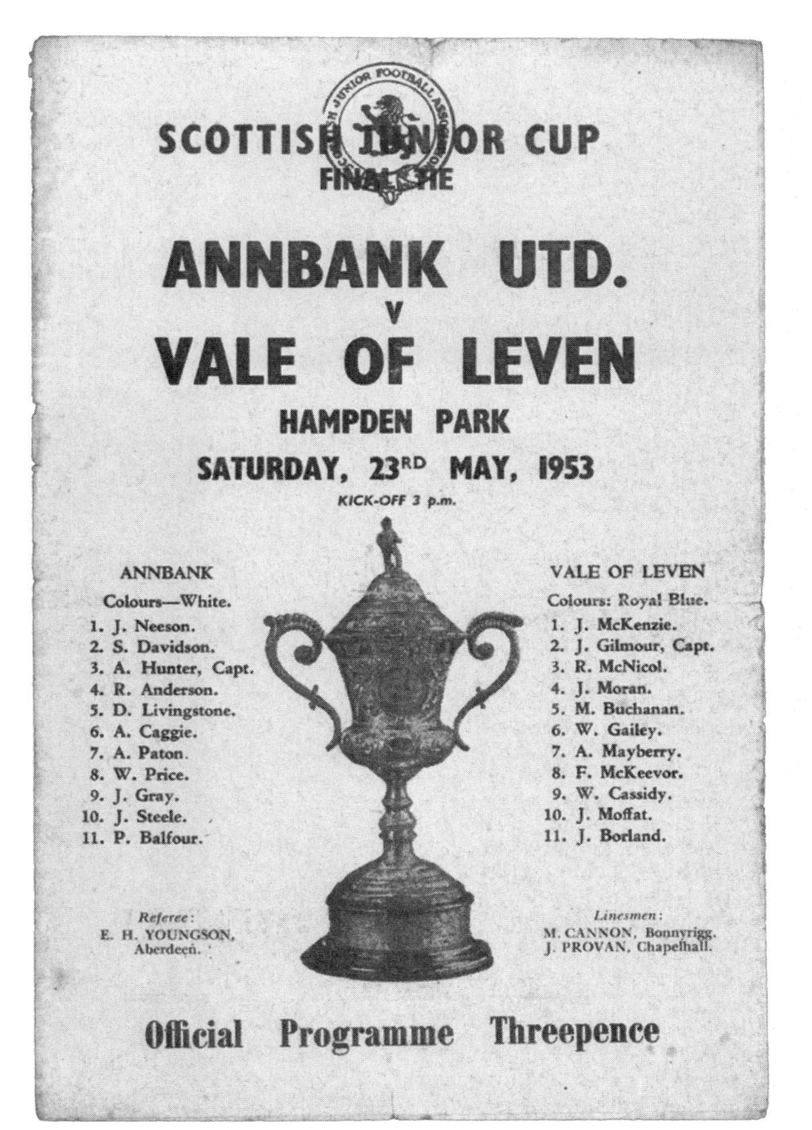

SCOTTISH JUNIOR CUP
FINAL TIE

ANNBANK UTD.
v
VALE OF LEVEN

HAMPDEN PARK

SATURDAY, 23RD MAY, 1953

KICK-OFF 3 p.m.

ANNBANK	VALE OF LEVEN
Colours—White.	Colours: Royal Blue.
1. J. Neeson.	1. J. McKenzie.
2. S. Davidson.	2. J. Gilmour, Capt.
3. A. Hunter, Capt.	3. R. McNicol.
4. R. Anderson.	4. J. Moran.
5. D. Livingstone.	5. M. Buchanan.
6. A. Caggie.	6. W. Gailey.
7. A. Paton.	7. A. Mayberry.
8. W. Price.	8. F. McKeevor.
9. J. Gray.	9. W. Cassidy.
10. J. Steele.	10. J. Moffat.
11. P. Balfour.	11. J. Borland.

Referee:
E. H. YOUNGSON, Aberdeen.

Linesmen:
M. CANNON, Bonnyrigg.
J. PROVAN, Chapelhall.

Official Programme Threepence

During the twentieth century a pipe band featured locally at different times and in different guises, making appearances at many and varied events. In July 1942 the district pipe band held its first tartan carnival in a packed New Hall, Annbank. The band performed under Pipe-Major Robert McCroskie, while Band-Sergeant Archibald McCroskie accompanied Highland dancers. Bessie Aitken was judged to be Tartan Queen with Annie Brodie a close second. The war years interrupted the band's progress and it was a reformed pipe band which entertained fans at Somerset Park, Ayr, in May 1949. Three months later they played to spectators at the opening of New Pebble Park. In July 1952 a crowd of over 10,000 attended the World Pipe Band Championships held in Somerset Park where Annbank Pipe Band were among the 1,500 pipers and drummers who took part in the massed band parade. The band used to play on Sunday afternoons on the lawn in front of Annbank House. This 1950s group of bandsmen features:
Back row: J. Smillie, _____, W. Saunders, A. Clark, W. Smillie, _____, J. McCallum
Front row: C. Riddick, W. Withers, G. Mossie, J. Clark, J. Riddick

With the local collieries closing, the band changed its home and name becoming the Killoch Colliery Pipe Band. Funding changed also with miners making voluntary contributions from their wage packets. The catchment area for members changed too. In this picture, resplendent in their tartan outfits, are:
J. McCroskie (Pipe-Major), R. Redmond, _____,
J. Callan, R. McPike, A. McPike, J. Clark, J. Hodge,
I. McCroskie, T. Graham, I. Drummond,
J. McCallum
Kneeling: H. Smillie, J. McCroskie, D. Drummond